One Hundred Years of Progress

ONE HUNDRED YEARS OF PROGRESS

by

Raymond Forsyth and Joseph Hagwood

Library of Congress Catalog Card No. 96-83760
ISBN 0-9652279-0-1

Cover design and photograph enhancements:
Erik Jon Mickelsen – EJM Designs, Sacramento, CA

Graphic design, typography and photograph enhancements:
Debbi Tempel & Troy Retzloff – Tempel Typographics, Sacramento, CA

The typefaces used in this book are
ITC New Baskerville, Gill Sans and Nuptial Script.

Editing:
Dierdre Honnold – Wordwrights International, Sacramento, CA

Printed by:
Signature Press, Sacramento, CA

California Transportation Foundation
P.O. Box 163453
Sacramento, California 95816

CONTENTS

Dedication vi

Foreword vii

Preface ix

Acknowledgements xi

1 PROLOGUE 1

2 BEGINNINGS 11

3 PROGRESS AND DEPRESSION 31

4 THE FREEWAY ERA 71

5 THE ENVIRONMENTAL AND
MULTI-MODAL ERA 127

Epilogue 163

Dedicated to the people of California and the visionaries who planned, designed and constructed one of the world's greatest transportation systems.

FOREWORD

The past one hundred years have encompassed spectacular achievement in the development of California's transportation system. Before the turn of the century, virtually all travel in the state was by horse-drawn vehicles or bicycle. The few existing roads were unpaved and often impassable. Today, California enjoys the most felicitous freeway system in the world, plus high speed rail and several urban light rail systems.

Such development was initiated in 1895 by the Legislature through the creation of the Bureau of Highways. The first act in the process was an inventory of existing roads by the three commissioners in two buckboards, thus generating a preliminary plan for a state highway system.

Authors Raymond Forsyth and Joseph Hagwood have captured such development in a photographic essay of over 270 pictures, many of which have never previously been published. "One Hundred Years of Progress" fills an important niche in California's history.

I congratulate the California Transportation Foundation for undertaking the publication of this landmark book.

Quentin L. Kopp
Chairman, Senate Transportation Committee
California Legislature

PREFACE

The following is a photographic essay on the development of the California transportation system. This project was begun by the California Transportation Foundation to mark the hundredth anniversary of the forerunner of Caltrans, the Bureau of Highways. The focal point of the essay, then, is the California Department of Transportation as it evolved. However, while this organization was a critically important factor in California transportation history, the contributions of other entities were, to say the least, substantial in the development of one of the world's greatest transportation systems. These include a generally supportive Legislature, the contractors who actually built it, the citizens' groups that actively promoted it, and the Federal Highway Administration which contributed so much to its success.

It is important to note that this is not a definitive history, but rather an attempt to capture pictorially and verbally some of the highlights of California's transportation history. In reviewing the literally thousands of available photographs, no real effort was made in the selection process to achieve balance. This would have been almost impossible in consideration of the hundred year time frame and the extreme diversity of the subject matter. Rather, selection was made based upon the story told and visual impact. In carrying out this assignment, I was moved by the vision, will and vitality of the men and women who planned, designed and constructed this state's transportation system. It is my sincere hope that this has been captured by the photographs selected.

Raymond A. Forsyth

ACKNOWLEDGEMENTS

The California Transportation Foundation wishes to acknowledge the contributions made by the companies or organizations and individuals listed below. The celebration of 100 years of transportation development in California has been made possible by their generous support.

CORPORATE SPONSORS

Operating Engineers Local Union No. 3
California State Employees Association
DeLeuw Cather & Company
Boyle Engineering Corporation
F.C.I. Constructors
Parsons Brinkerhoff
Sverdrup Corporation
H.D.R. Engineering Inc.
General Motors Corporation

Fluor Daniel Inc.
Madonna Construction Co.
Quarter Century Club – Central District
Minnesota Mining and Manufacturing Co.
Wells Fargo Bank
Signature Press
Greiner Inc. Pacific
Johnson and Associates

INDIVIDUALS

Don Alden
Larry Bishop
Margaret Buss
Edith Darknell
Bob Flock
James Greathead

Louise Hess
Arthur Kreiger
David Mast
Charles Pivetti
Ernest K. Parke

Lynn Protteau
Norman Root
Travis Smith
Joseph Thomas
Larry Wieman

The authors would also like to acknowledge and thank the California Department of Transportation for its cooperation and assistance in the development of "One Hundred Years of Progress." Staff members within the department providing valuable assistance and information included Laurel Clark, Edith Darknell, Patti Ehret, Rudy Hendrix, Mary Hicks, Fred Jager, Terri Kinney, Diane Johnson, Rogel Prysock, Dr. Clifford Roblee, Norman Root, Roger Stoughton, and Dale Williams.

Don Alden and Bob Cassano provided very useful input on those portions of the essay concerned with structures. The services of Peter Asano, former Chief of the Caltrans Photo Lab, were vital to the extent that the project would not have been possible without his participation. Thanks also to those who helped get this project "on the road," through personal loans and to others who helped in various ways.

Finally, great credit should be given to Larry Wieman of the California Transportation Foundation for his dogged determination to complete the project in the face of any number of obstacles.

CHAPTER 1

PROLOGUE
1769-1894

"Oh, if these mountains could only talk, they would tell you tales and ghostlike stories that would haunt you to the grave."

Emigrant John Wood – Carson Pass – 1850

In the late 1760s, the Spanish government was becoming increasingly concerned over English and Russian encroachments into northern California. Consequently, it was decided to implement a plan which had been under consideration for some time, the colonization of California by Spanish citizens. This decision was enthusiastically supported by Father Junipero Serra, President of the Lower California Missions, who had an abiding interest in establishing a chain of Franciscan missions for the spiritual pacification of Alta California.

At a conference in 1768 between Serra and a representative of the Spanish government, San Diego was selected as the location of the first settlement and mission. Governor Don Gaspar de Portola was selected to lead the land expedition into the heretofore unexplored northern region of California.

In March, 1769 a party consisting of soldiers, colonists, and servants with livestock and flocks departed from Loreto in Lower California with Portola and Serra in charge. After a difficult journey of nearly two months, the expedition arrived in San Diego where they were reprovisioned by two awaiting ships.

Serra remained in San Diego to begin the mission while Portola and sixty-four soldiers pushed on in an effort to find Monterey Harbor which had been described in glowing terms by an earlier explorer (Vizcaino) from his voyage along the California coast in 1602. Portola returned after an arduous six months, having discovered San Francisco Bay although unsuccessful in his quest for Monterey Harbor. After resupply, Portola set out once more to find the elusive harbor and was ultimately successful. In June, 1770, Father Serra began work on the second mission, San Carlos Borromeo de Monterey. By 1783, seven additional missions were established. The trail connecting them was named by Portola "El Camino Real," the Royal Road, later to become U.S. 101 and State Route 1.

Between 1774 and 1776, an overland route from northern Mexico to California was established by Juan Bautista de Anza from Sonora to Monterey. His trail across what is now the Imperial Valley, ultimately became the Sonora Road, Colorado Road, the Emigrant Trail and the Butterfield Stage Route. Anza's trail in San Diego and Imperial counties closely approximates portions of State Routes 78, 79, and 60.

In 1822, upon achieving independence from Spain, Mexico relaxed foreign trade restrictions in California. Famed mountain man Jedediah Smith strongly suspected the region to be rich in fur, particularly beaver. On August 22, 1826, Smith mounted an exploratory expedition from the Great Salt Lake consisting of fifteen mountain men with fifty horses and proceeded southwesterly across the Colorado River, ultimately reaching what is now Needles. After reprovisioning, the party crossed the San Bernardino mountains, possibly through Cajon Pass, stopping again at Mission San Gabriel. After Smith was denied permission by Mexican authorities to trap beaver, the party ultimately crossed the coast range into Oregon. Other trappers and traders followed including Joseph Walker who, in 1833, was the first American to penetrate California through the Sierra Nevada mountains. The paths and trails found by these intrepid mountain men were ultimately to be the basis of much of the present day highway system.

In the 1840s, interest in California was stimulated by the descriptions contained in the books by Richard Henry Dana ("Two Years Before the Mast") and Jefferson Farnam ("Life and Adventures in California"). The U.S. government sponsored several expeditions into California including that headed by Lieutenant John C. Fremont of the Corps of Topographical Engineers in 1843. Fremont was destined to play a key role in securing California for the United States during the war with Mexico three years later.

The lure of California stimulated emigration by wagon train as early as 1841. The Bidwell-Bartelson party reached the San Joaquin valley via Walker Pass with great difficulty that same year. In 1844, the High Sierra was initially penetrated by wagon train by the Stevens-Murphy-Townsend party which followed the Truckee river and crossed over what is now Donner Summit. The Donner party disaster (1846) was the last attempt over this traill until after the Mexican war.

California was ceded to the United States by Mexico at the war's conclusion under the terms of the treaty of Guadalupe Hidalgo on February 2, 1848. Just two weeks later, the discovery of gold at Sutter's sawmill triggered the mass migration to California commonly referred to as the "gold rush". The initial influx of gold seekers came to California by sea. However, in the spring of 1849, thousands of emigrants began moving westward by wagon. Eighteen thousand crossed the Missouri river in a three week period. Those wagon trains seeking to enter northern California across the Sierra would generally rendezvous at Truckee Meadows (Reno) from which the crossing would be made following the Truckee through Donner Pass. For those whose destination was the Feather River basin, a northwesterly route through Beckworth Pass was used. Another commonly used route followed the West Walker River crossing the Sierra a few miles south of Sonora Pass.

Almost immediately after statehood was granted in 1850, Californians began to apply political pressure for improved roads. Petitions were submitted from a number of cities and towns to this effect prompting the Legislature to finally act in 1855. The provisions of a bill signed on April 28 of that year called for the construction of a wagon road from the Sacramento Valley over the Sierra to the state's eastern border at a cost "not to exceed $105,000". Unfortunately, the Legislature failed to appropriate the funds to do so. Because the lack of legislative support, a policy of granting franchises evolved for building toll roads or improving those few already in existence. A number of toll roads and bridges were built throughout California between 1850 and 1880, particularly in mountainous areas. Some yielded handsome profits to their entreprenurial builders while others washed out in the first winter floods at great financial loss. Thus, the "Lake Tahoe Wagon Road" was constructed as a toll road by private investors in 1858. Eventually, the state, through legislative authorization, acquired the road from the El Dorado County Board of Supervisors in 1895. This heavily trafficked facility on the site of present day Route 50, became the first state highway.

A successful Trans-Sierra toll road came into being as the result of the construction of the transcontinental railroad (1861-1869). In 1864 the "Big Four" of the Central Pacific constructed the Dutch Flat and Donner Lake Wagon Road over the Sierra in support of railroad construction. The ninety mile long road was begun in the fall of 1862 and completed in June 1864. During its relatively brief existence, this facility captured much of the trans Sierra stage and freight business so that a good deal of the original investment in it was recovered. In addition, it has been estimated that its existence saved a year of railroad construction time for the Central Pacific, which meant significant additional land subsidies from the government since the meeting with the United Pacific occurred at Promontory Point, Utah rather than the eastern California border as originally anticipated.

Some of these toll roads were well located and constructed. The high rock retaining walls built by Chinese laborers for the wagon road into Sierra County are a monument to the skill and energy of these pioneer builders. Similarly, some very ingenious and well constructed bridges were built such as the timber covered bridges, constructed by emigrants from New England, the wire suspension bridges constructed by Andrew Hallidie who apprenticed under John Roebling of Brooklyn Bridge fame, and the stone arch bridges, generally built by European trained stonecutters.

Built first for freight traffic, many of these roads were also used by a number of stage companies whose Concord stagecoaches criss-crossed the state. However, the roads were generally built to serve a specific market, usually connecting a port to a mining district. It was not until after 1895 that these scattered elements began to be integrated into a statewide road system.

Mission San Diego de Alcala founded by Father Junipero Serra in 1769.

The only authentic portrait of Father Junipero Serra, founder of the California missions, painted in Mexico City in 1773. The El Camino Real, built to connect all 19 missions, was California's first road system.

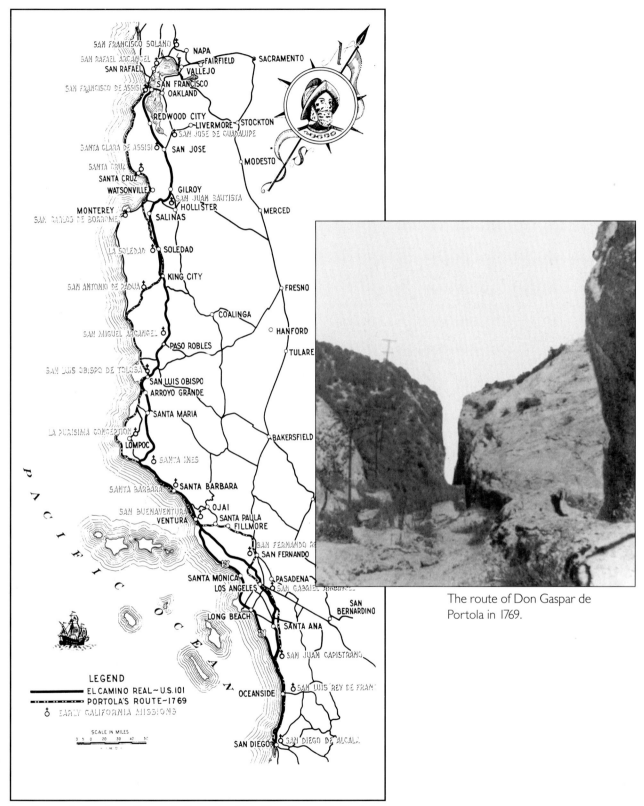

The route of Don Gaspar de Portola in 1769.

San Fernando Pass from the south through which Don Gaspar de Portola passed in 1769. Originally a 12' cut made by the early Spaniards, it was deepened to 80' by the U.S. Army under the command of General Beale in the mid 19th century.

Captain Joseph Walker and his wife, circa 1837. Painting by Alfred Jacob Miller courtesy of the Joslyn Art Museum, Omaha, Nebraska.

"Jedediah Smith in the Badlands" by Harvey Dunn. South Dakota Art Museum Collection, Brookings, South Dakota.

Old woodcut of the emigrant wagon toll road from Lake Tahoe to Placerville from the book "Down the Sierras in 1865".

"Rough Going over the Sierras" by Harold Von Schmidt. Dismantling a wagon to surmount Donner Pass. Courtesy John Morrell & Co., Cincinatti, Ohio

DUTCH FLAT WAGON ROAD.

This new route over the Mountains, by way of Dutch Flat and Donner Lake, can now be traveled by Teams without load, and will be open for loaded Teams

JUNE 15th, 1864.

IT IS

The Shortest, Best and Cheapest Route to Washoe, Humboldt and Reese River.

Its grade going East at no place exceeds ten inches to the rod, and it is wide enough for Two Teams to pass without difficulty   All teams coming West, without load, can travel the New Road FREE OF TOLL, until further notice.   All those taking loads at Newcastle, the terminus of the Central Pacific Railroad, three miles from Auburn, can travel the New Road going East, Free of Toll, up to July 1, 1864.

Teams starting from Virginia City will take the Henness Pass Road to Ingram's, at Sardine Valley, where the New Road turns off to the left.

CHARLES CROCKER

Sacramento, June 6, 1864   Pres't of the Co.

A flyer demonstrating the business acumen of Charles Crocker, president of the Central Pacific Railroad, encouraging freight haulers to use the road constructed in support of the transcontinental railroad free of toll for approximately two weeks.

The beginning of the celebration of the completion of the transcontinental railroad immediately after driving the golden spike at Promontary Point, Utah on May 10, 1869. The Andrew J. Russell Collection, The Oakland Museum of California.

The Lake Tahoe Wagon Road, originally constructed as a toll road in 1858. It was acquired by the State in 1895, becoming the first state highway.

Patterson Grade on the Sonora and Mono Toll Road in 1897.

CHAPTER 2

BEGINNINGS
1895-1918

"The fact is, that the industrial development of our State has nearly reached the limit possible with bad roads. If it is to progress further, it must have, as a basis, the economic and systematic administration of highway affairs."

R.C. Irvine, et al. – 1896

In spite of the efforts of such dedicated State Surveyor Generals as H.S. Marlette and John A. Brewster, California's road construction and maintenance had languished from the State's admission to the Union in 1850 until the late 1800s, due to a continuing shortage of funds and the presence of incompetent or self-serving office holders in control of the State's development.

In response to a growing concern over the perceived inadequacy of the surface transportation system by the public, and pressure from special interest groups such as the "League of American Wheelmen" (bicycle enthusiasts), the Legislature, in 1895, created the Bureau of Highways, consisting of three men appointed by the governor. They were Marsden Manson (who had a reputation as one of California's foremost engineers), R.C. Irvine, and J.L. Maude. They described the situation in their first annual report (1896) as follows:

"The condition of highways in California today is the result of generations of neglect and apathy. Not only has this been the case, but an unfortunate outgrowth of our system of government has permitted the injection of politics into the business of management of economic matters of great importance... In too many instances, the road funds have been regarded as the funds from which to pay political debts."

The commissioners proceeded to inventory the existing road system by horse-drawn buckboard. In the course of their review, they logged in excess of 16,500 miles compiling information on the topographic and geologic features of each county, availability of water, stone quarries and gravel deposits and laws in force pertaining to highways.

In their report to the governor, submitted November 25, 1896, the commissioners recommended a system of state highways made up of twenty eight separate routes. The skill and vision of this group is attested to by the fact that the existing state highway system corresponds closely to that recommended in the 1896 report.

In 1897, the Legislature dissolved the Bureau of Highways and established the Department of Highways consisting of three commissioners appointed for two year terms and a civil engineer for four years. J.L. Maude of the original bureau was appointed by the governor to the latter position.

As a result of the work of the Bureau (subsequently the Department) of Highways, the State Constitution was amended on November 4, 1902, giving the Legislature the power to establish a system of state highways and to pass the laws necessary for highway construction and to extend state aid to counties for their road systems.

However, despite the constitutional amendment, the legal basis for highway development proved to be inadequate. This plus local politics resulted in little real progress.

In 1907, the Legislature dissolved the Department of Highways and created the Department of Engineering, the forerunner of the Department of Public Works. Highway funding was provided by the Legislature through "Special Appropriations" administered by the Department of Engineering. Because of a minimal funding level, available resources were devoted, for the most part, to clearing debris from winter storms and the construction of culverts, retaining walls and bridges. The slow pace of progress in the development of an adequate highway system and the critical need for it became readily apparent to the Legislature and public.

In response, the Legislature passed an act providing for an $18,000,000 bond issue in 1909 which was approved by the voters the following year. It required that the Department of Engineering acquire the necesary land and construct a continuous and connected highway system.

The Chandler Act, passed by the Legislature in 1911, authorized the appointment of a three member advisory board to the Department of Engineering which was to become the first Highway Commission. The Act also provided for the appointment of a State Highway Engineer to serve at the pleasure of the governor. The first of these was Austin B. Fletcher, an individual with a national reputation in highway matters, and, as it developed, an obvious talent for management and organization.

Based upon a 6800 mile tour of the state's road system by Fletcher and the commissioners in 1911 and the results of earlier studies, the Highway Commission adopted a state highway system. Based upon Fletcher's recommendation, the state was divided into seven "Divisions" (now Districts) each in the charge of an experienced engineer. On January 2, 1912, the seven Division Engineers began their work.

On August 7, 1912, Commission Chairman Burton Towne turned the first shovel of earth for State Highway Contract No. 1 for a section of the coast route between South San Francisco and Burlingame. This same year, the Commission authorized the construction of a materials testing facility at the State Fair grounds. This 16' by 16' building was the forerunner of what was to become known as the Transportation Laboratory.

The year 1914 saw the beginnings of the present Caltrans Maintenance function, supported by funds made available by a 1913 legislative act requiring motor vehicle registration. Revenue generated by vehicle registration fees were to be divided between the state and counties which made it possible to develop a systematic maintenance program for highways under state jurisdiction.

When it became apparent that the funds from the 1910 bond issue were woefully inadequate for completion of the adopted highway system, an additional $15,000,000 bond issue was approved in 1916.

The 1915 Legislature also passed the "Convict Labor Law" by which the Department of Engineering was permitted to utilize prison labor for highway construction. Subsequently roads, particularly in remote areas, were constructed by convict labor for many years to come.

The Federal Aid program was initiated with the enactment of the Bankhead Act by Congress in 1916. California received $151,063.92 in Federal Aid funds for the fiscal year ending June 30, 1917.

Several important highway projects were completed by 1918, including the Ridge Route, which cut the distance between Bakersfield and Los Angeles by fifty miles and the Yolo Causeway which provided an all weather link between Sacramento and San Francisco. Other projects of significance were the Kings River Canyon, Alturas-Cedarville, Emigrant Gap, and Imperial County plank roads.

Bureau of Highway Commissioners
J.L. Maude, R.C. Irvine (with camera)
and their dog "Maje" in the process of
inventorying the existing road using a
buckboard and horses in 1896. Over 7000
miles were traversed in this manner for
the Bureau's study.

Minutes of the first
meeting of the
Bureau of Highways,
April 11, 1895.

Department of Highways cook and equipment wagon, 1900.

Map prepared by the Bureau of Highways in 1896 presenting their recommendation for a State Highway System.

An unsurfaced and poorly drained street in Vacaville at the turn of the century, a common sight during the winter and spring.

An oiled earth road between Winters and Davis, 1906.

The newly constructed Alturas-Cedarville Road on which grades of 6% replaced those of up to 20%, 1906.

Grading an oiled earth road in Yolo County, circa 1906.

Steam shovel at work on Kings River Canyon Road, circa 1907.

The Emigrant Gap Road in 1909 when taken over by the State from Placer and Nevada Counties.

State surveyors at work on El Camino Real in San Mateo County in 1911. Note the California Highway Commission (CHC) brand on the horse's shank. Draft animals were state issue in those days.

This picture with title was used in early bond issue campaign.

Reconnoitering for a State Highway in Humboldt County, circa 1912.

Chairman Towne of the Highway Commission turns the first shovel of earth for State Highway Contract No. I in San Mateo County, August 7, 1912.

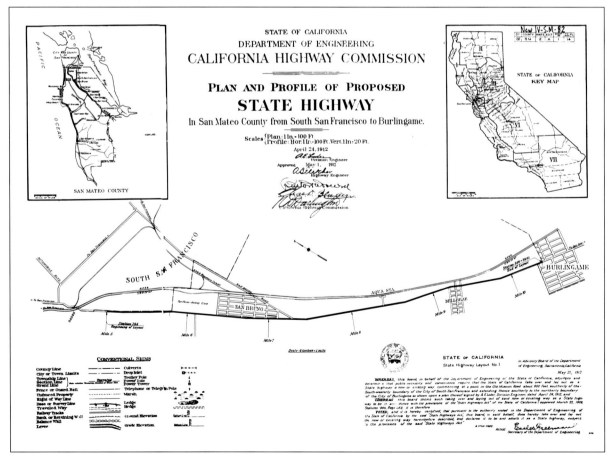

Plan cover sheet for Contract No. I dated April 24, 1912.

Rolling asphalt concrete surfacing on State Highway Contract No. 1 in San Mateo County in 1913.

A 1913 vintage survey party and camp.

State highway surveyors moving camp, Rattlesnake Creek, Mendocino County ,circa 1913.

Final rolling of aggregate base prior to surfacing on a state highway near Marysville, circa 1912.

"Saving the Trees": an early example of environmental concerns versus traffic safety on a state highway near Roseville, circa 1913.

State highway traffic counters start to work in 1913.

Grading the Calabasas–Ventura Highway over Canejo grade with Fresno scrapers, a California invention, 1913.

Early U.S. Bureau of Public Roads sponsored concrete pavement research. Testing a 4" concrete pavement slab with a Kelly Springfield roller in 1913.

Cautionary sign on a state highway construction project, circa 1914.

State highway construction in El Dorado County, 1914.

Convicts being returned to camp after a day's work on a state highway project, circa 1915.

A construction mishap on a highway construction project (US 101) near Cloverdale in Sonoma County, 1914.

Surveying in the Sacramento Canyon at Dog Creek for a state highway in 1916.

"Old Plank Road" built in 1915-1916 in Imperial County. With room for one vehicle, turnouts were provided at half mile intervals, and drivers were expected to sound air horns to warn oncoming motorists of their presence. Improved as an oiled earth road in 1924, it eventually became Interstate 8.

Convicts at work on the Mendocino-Humboldt Highway, 1916. Much of the State Highway construction with convict labor was by hand.

Placement of concrete pavement on Belmont Avenue in Fresno, 1916.

A tough setup by surveyors working in Shasta County near Castle Craigs, circa 1916.

Bridge over the Pit River in Shasta County. Completed in 1916, this structure was built at a cost of $37,000. Its reinforced concrete arch span length of 242 feet was the longest in California at the time. This site is now submerged under Shasta Lake.

Motorized asphalt distributor on a state highway project in Los Angeles County, 1913.

A reinforced concrete arch bridge with a 180' long center span and two spans of 114' over the Sacramento River at Dunsmuir. Designed for Siskiyou County by the firm of Noland and Sarter, it was constructed in 1917 by the California Highway Commission at a cost of $45,000. This bridge is still in service as part of I-5.

Ridge Route between Bakersfield and Los Angeles, 1916. The sum of all curves on the route equaled 110 full circles.

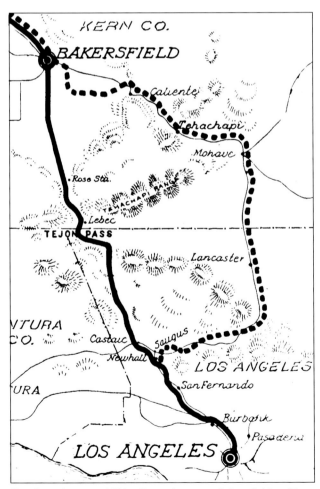

Plan for a shortened Ridge Route between Bakersfield and Los Angeles, 1916. The prior route is shown by the dotted line.

110' cut on the Ridge Route near Castaic, 1916.

The Yolo Basin concrete trestle. Three miles in length, it was completed in 1916 at a cost of $400,000 thus providing the first year round highway access across the Sacramento Valley in the 120 miles between Rio Vista and Marysville.

An overloaded rice truck and trailer in Colusa County, circa 1917. The extensive and severe pavement problems caused by overloading trucks, particularly in northern Sacramento County, prompted the enactment of truck weight limits in the Motor Vehicle Act of 1917.

CHAPTER 3

PROGRESS AND DEPRESSION 1919-1939

"To be a builder is a great thing. To be a BUILDER OF CALIFORNIA should be sufficient to enthrall the imagination, arouse the ambition and enlist the energy and the efforts of everyone to whom has been given the privilege of such service."

B.B. Meek, Director of Public Works,
State of California – 1927

The years between 1919 and 1939 were pivotal in the development of California's transportation system. Organizational changes and the development of a stable and predictable funding source resulted in an accelerated highway and bridge construction program despite the onset of the "great depression" in the early 1930's.

The 1919 legislature amended the Motor Vehicle Act of 1913 by requiring that county supervisors submit an annual report detailing the expenditure of road funds derived from the state Motor Vehicle Fund. This was done to assure that these funds were expended in accordance with the intent of the original legislation.

In the special election of July 1, 1919, the people of California approved a third, and as it was developed, a final highway construction bond for $40,000,000 bringing the total to $73,000,000 as of that date. However, the deficiencies of this "fits and starts" method of funding highway construction were beginning to be recognized by both the Highway Commission and the Legislature. In its 1919-1920 Biennial Report, the Commission initially recommended a tax on gasoline to fund highway construction while the 1921-1922 report warned of the rapid depletion of bond funds. A consensus was developing in favor of "pay as you go" highway financing, i.e., a gasoline tax which was finally enacted by the 1923 Legislature. Under its provisions, a two cent per gallon tax was imposed with 1 cent dedicated to the construction of state highways and the remainder to the counties for road improvement purposes.

In a major organizational change, the 1921 legislature created the Department of Public Works which included the Highway Commission, the State Water Commission and the newly created Division of Highways. In 1923, the Highway Commission became a separate state agency largely responsible for the highway matters previously handled by the Department of Public Works. This same year the Commission created three new "Divisions" (Districts) with offices in Stockton, Bishop and San Bernardino.

Until 1923, due to funding constraints, the Highway Commission required that counties provide right-of-way, designs, and construction funding for the bridges needed for most new State Highways. Because this arrangement proved to be unsatisfactory, State Highway Engineer R.M. Morton, in 1923, directed that all State Highway bridges be designed and their construction overseen by state engineers. This policy change resulted in the creation of the Bridge Department (now the Division of Structures).

A key piece of Legislation enacted in 1925, the Melville Act, provided that the state take over all traversable highways, abolish toll roads, and build highways through small cities which could not otherwise afford them. In effect, the responsibility of the Division of Highways was extended beyond rural highway construction. The act also provided that the Highway Commission could relinquish roads with the consent of the local governing body.

The 1927 legislature reconstituted the Department of Public Works to consist of four divisions, including the Division of Highways. The State Highway Engineer was placed in charge of the Division of Highways. The Highway Commission, which remained a separate entity, was expanded to five members. It was given the power to alter state highway routes, abandon unneeded sections, and condemn rights of way.

The same year, the legislature enacted the Breed Bill which placed an additional one cent tax on gasoline, the proceeds of which were to be exclusively used for new highway construction.

The 1929 Legislature created the California Toll Bridge Authority, which was authorized to acquire or construct and operate toll bridges within the state and to issue bonds for this purpose. Ultimately, the acquisition, operation and construction of toll bridges was vested with the Department of Public Works.

The 1933 legislature amended the State Highway Classification Act of 1927 adding 6700 miles of county roads to the State Highway System. Highway construction funds were allocated equally between primary and secondary highways. In response to the additional work load resulting from this legislation, an eleventh district was established with headquarters in San Diego. The legislative and organizational changes of 1923-1933 thus provided the basis for an unprecedented level of highway and bridge construction activity in subsequent years.

With the onset of the "Great Depression" in 1929, the Department of Public Works made a concerted effort to relieve unemployment by the establishment of highway relief camps throughout the state which employed thousands for highway maintenance work. Preference in hiring was given to men with families in order to maximize the benefits of the program. Works Progress Administration (WPA) and relief workers were also used extensively on individual highway and bridge construction projects.

Preeminent among the many projects constructed during this period was the San Francisco-Oakland Bay Bridge. This eight and one quarter mile long combination steel truss suspension bridge and tunnel was planned and constructed by the San Francisco-Oakland Bay Bridge Division of the Department of Public Works under the direction of State Highway Engineer C.H. Purcell. Funding was provided by the issuance of revenue bonds by the California Toll Bridge Authority. Begun in 1931, the bridge was completed and opened in November 1936, at a cost of approximately $70,000,000.

The Golden Gate Bridge, which became a major San Francisco landmark, was completed in 1937. The main suspended span, with a length of 4200 feet, was the longest in the world until the completion of New York City's Verrazano Bridge in 1964. Although it carries State Route 101 traffic, it was designed, constructed, maintained, and is still owned by a separate public entity, the Golden Gate Bridge, Highway and Transportation District.

Other noteworthy projects included highways in the Feather River Canyon, San Marcos Pass, the Ridge Route, Cuesta Grade, the Bayshore Highway, Meyer's Grade, the approaches to the Golden Gate Bridge, and portions of the Coast Highway. Landmark structures completed included the Bixby Creek and Tower ("M" Street) Bridges and the Yolo Causeway widening. A project with great future significance was begun in 1936, the construction of California's first freeway, the Arroyo Seco Parkway.

The 1919-1939 era was one of significant technological advancement in transportation in California. The Pittsburg Test Highway sponsored jointly by the U.S. Bureau of Public Roads and the California Highway Commission (1920-1922) yielded significant results in the design of rigid pavements. Advances were made in erosion control and landscape architecture. Truck weighing and load control were initiated. The 1930's saw the first use of reflectorized signs, divided highways and concrete traffic safety barriers.

Convict labor at work on a state
highway in Mendocino County,
circa 1920.

Luther Burbank planting the
first tree on the state highway
between Santa Rosa and
Petaluma, March, 1921.

Loaded trucks at the Pittsburg Road Test conducted by U.S. Bureau of Public Roads and the California Highway Commission from 1920 to 1922. Several modifications in concrete pavement design practice resulted from this effort.

Trucks loaded to 50 tons for the Pittsburg Road Test.

Newly constructed California Highway Commission Shops in Sacramento, circa 1921. With a floor area of 26,000 square feet, this facility was fully equipped for overhauling all commission equipment. Surplus army trucks given to the states after World War I by the government provided the beginnings of the commission's motorized fleet.

Traffic regulation inspectors of the California Highway Commission check out a suspected truck overload with portable scales, circa 1921.

The Auburn-Verdi road (now I-80) blocked
by 4000 sheep in 1922, a common problem
for early motorists.

Sidehill viaduct along the Eel River on a state highway in Mendocino County, 1924. The extremely steep terrain at the site would have required the removal of large quantities of rock for conventional road construction. The horizontal shelf is tied to rock and supported on its outer edge by reinforced concrete columns.

Grade separation and bridge over the Susan River on a state highway in Lassen County. This 248' long structure consists of a 100' two rib open spandrel arch and a series of 15' approach spans. It was completed in January, 1924.

Experimental plank road construction across the sand
hills in Imperial County, 1924.

The Donner Summit Bridge and commemorative plaque dedicated in September, 1927 in the presence of descendants of the Donner Party. With an overall length of 241' including a 110' arch with a depth of 70', the structure made possible a 7% grade from Donner Lake to the summit, eliminating the 18-20% grades of the old road.

A District 8, San Bernardino maintenance man clearing boulders from a state highway in attire considered appropriate for temperatures hovering around 120 degrees F., 1927.

A "super earthmover" being demonstrated by the Kaiser Paving Co. on a widening project in San Mateo County in 1927. The telescoping earthmover invented by R.E. Letourneau had a capacity of 15 cubic yards.

"Mrs. Hauser and the Elephant": An unusual and ultimately costly problem presented to the Hauser Construction Co. while working on the Redwood Highway near Orick: the disposal of a dead circus elephant, 1927.

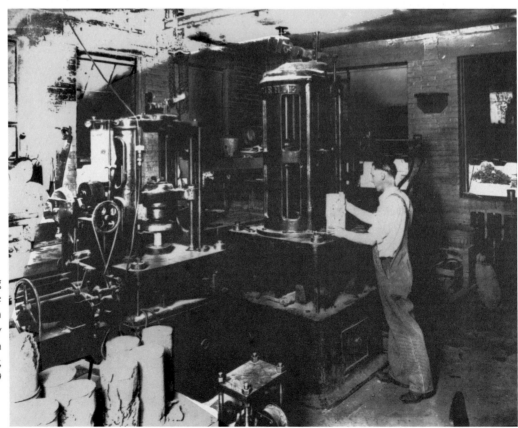

Testing concrete cylinders in the highway commission laboratory, 1929

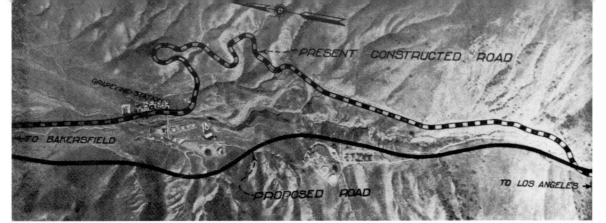

Plan for the relocation of the Grapevine Grade portion of the Ridge Route which eliminated 95 curves and maintained a maximum 6% grade along its 11.6 mile length, 1932.

Final grading of the seven-mile Ridge Route Alternate which was completed in July 1931 at a cost of approximately $650,000.

Dedication of the Ridge Route Alternate on October 29, 1933. The new facility, built at a cost of $2,864,000, required 4 years to build. Requiring 4,252,000 cubic yards of excavation, it shortened the length of the Ridge Route by 10 miles and increased the minimum radius of curvature from 70' to 1000'.

Bridge at Pulga in the Feather River Canyon, under construction in January, 1932. The steel arch, which spans both the river and an existing railroad bridge, is 680' in length 200' above the river.

Work gang of Relief Employment Camp G in Plumas County pulling a compressor uphill on a highway construction project (Rte. 70) in 1932.

The old and the new. The decrepit and narrow (15') bridge over the Salinas River (top) replaced by a new steel truss structure with a concrete deck in 1932 at a cost of approximately $275,000. The new bridge was 1666' in length with a roadway width of 24'. It is still in service as a county road.

Scenes from the construction of the Bixby Creek bridge on the coast route between Carmel and San Simeon in 1932. The open spandrel concrete arch was a record breaking 330' in length.

Dedication of the Bixby Creek Bridge on November 28, 1932. At the far right is Acting Bridge Engineer F.W. Panhorst, under whose direction the longest single span concrete arch to that time (330') was designed. To Panhorst's right are District 05 Engineer Lester Gibson, J.W. Howe, Secretary of the Highway Commission, L.V. Campbell, State Highway Office Engineer, T.M. Reardon, State Highway Commissioner, Audrey Mawdsley (cutting), E. Tickle, Senator-elect, A.A. Caruthers, Supervisor, and R.M. Dorton, Monterey City Manager.

An early and somewhat primitive pavement drilling rig capable of recovering 5" diameter cores for testing and inspection, 1932.

Miss Myrtle V. Murray was sworn in as Interim Director of the Department of Public Works on October 10, 1932. "She is indispensable," agreed Governor Rolph in recognition of her service as secretary to five governors and six directors. The department's first woman director resigned several days later upon the appointment of Earl Lee Kelly as Director for whom she became Administrative Assistant and Secretary.

Four bridges under construction in Piru Gorge along the Ridge Route Alternative, 1933. This portion of the Ridge Route is now under Pyramid Reservoir.

Giant redwood brought down in Mendocino County to provide lumber for the Yolo Causeway project and employment to woodsmen and mill workers in Fort Bragg. This one was 18' in diameter and an estimated 2512 years in age. The estimated yield was 170,000 board feet, 1933.

An optimistic sign on a state highway project near Gold Run, 1932.

A newspaper cartoon celebrating the failure of a court challenge of the Outdoor Advertising Act passed by the legislature in 1933 which prohibited signs or structures within 300' of intersections not in subdivided areas or unincorporated sections of the state. The bill further prohibited signs and structures in an unsafe condition, in drainage channels, or obstructing the view of highways for 500 feet, 1934.

Director Earl Lee Kelly unlocks the barrier opening the improved Santa Monica Coast Highway along Palisades Beach on July 2, 1934.

A 100,000 cubic yard embankment on the San Marcos Pass realignment, between the coast highway and Santa Ynez, nears completion, 1935.

WPA workers at work on shoulder construction in Madera County, circa 1935

Easterly lift tower of the "M" Street Bridge in Sacramento under construction. Upper right, Governor Merriam inspects the work in progress, circa 1935.

Workers clinging, with the aid of ropes, to the precipitous face of Grizzly Dome while engaged in blasting and excavation work on East Portal Tunnel No. 2 for the new Feather River Highway. December 1935.

Where the Extra Load Should Be Shouldered!

Reprinted from the LOS ANGELES TIMES with permission

Newspaper cartoon in support of the proposed "Unification Plan" to shift the costs of local road maintenance and construction to the state gas fund, 1935.

Slides and washouts of the winter of 1935-1936. Top, slide removal in Trinity County. Center, San Marcos Pass closed by rock slides. Bottom, washout on the Van Duzen River, State Route 35.

Governor Rolph signs three bills constituting enabling legislation for the design and construction of the San Francisco-Oakland Bay Bridge on May 25, 1931. Project Chief Engineer C.H. Purcell (in dark rimmed glasses) stands behind the governor.

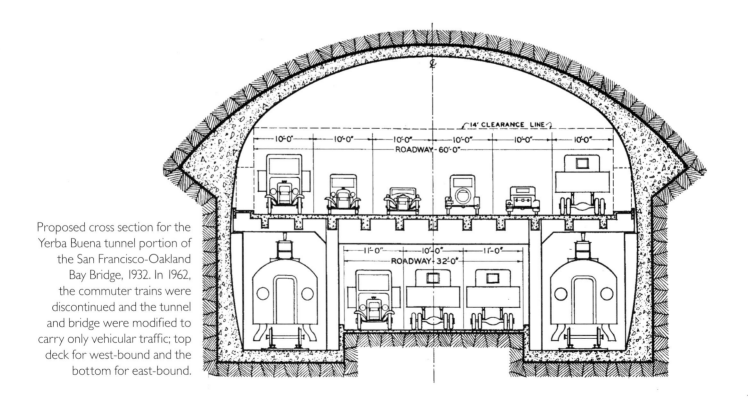

Proposed cross section for the Yerba Buena tunnel portion of the San Francisco-Oakland Bay Bridge, 1932. In 1962, the commuter trains were discontinued and the tunnel and bridge were modified to carry only vehicular traffic; top deck for west-bound and the bottom for east-bound.

Director Earl Lee Kelly applies his signature to one of six thousand San Francisco-Oakland Bay Bridge bonds ($1000 denomination) in 1933.

San Francisco-Oakland Bay Bridge construction. Pier W4 to San Francisco from the southeast, 1933.

San Francisco-Oakland Bay Bridge construction showing, in the foreground, pier foundations for the East Bay crossing to Yerba Buena Island and, in the background, completed towers extending from the island to San Francisco, 1935.

"Lifting Steel": San Francisco-Oakland Bay Bridge under construction, 1935.

Dedication of the San Francisco-Oakland Bay Bridge on November 12, 1936. Governor Merriam severs the gold chain barrier with a blow torch. From left to right, C.H. Purcell, Chief Engineer, Herbert Hoover, former President, Frank M. Merriam, Governor, C. Henderson, Director of the Reconstruction Finance Corporation, W.G. McAdoo, U.S. Senator, and E.L. Kelly, Director of Public Works.

PREVIOUS PAGE:
San Francisco-Oakland Bay Bridge from Yerba Buena Island
to San Francisco, completed, November, 1936.

Record rainfall in February, 1937 resulted in extensive flood damage to highways and bridges in southern California. Here, San Mateo Creek washes away pavement and shoulders 20 miles north of Oceanside in San Diego County.

Sketch shows course of State's approach to Golden Gate span from Waldo Point through tunnel to the bridge, May, 1937.

Scenes from the construction of the Marin County approach to the Golden Gate Bridge, including the "heading" for the Waldo Tunnel, 1937.

Interior view of the state-built Waldo Tunnel under construction on the Marin County approach to the Golden Gate Bridge, 1937. The Waldo approach, including the 1000' tunnel, was constructed at a cost of approximately $2,000,000.

The Golden Gate Bridge upon completion in May, 1937. The main center span was the longest single span (4200') of any suspension bridge in the world. View of the bridge from the San Francisco side.

East Portal Tunnel No. 2 at Grizzly Dome (Feather River Highway) as completed in August, 1937.

Scenes from the construction of the new Cuesta Grade (US 101) just north of San Luis Obispo. This 3.3 mile, 4 lane divided highway eliminated 59 curves, some of which were considered hazardous. The original alignment was built in 1915 and improved in 1923. August, 1937.

A multi-purpose foundation drill rig designed by engineers of the Materials and Research Foundation and built by the Equipment Department. Bottom right, a foundation inspector emerges from an 80' deep hole, a practice which would probably greatly trouble OSHA today. 1937.

Scenes at dedication of Lone Pine-Death Valley Highway. Upper, view of new highway leading down into Panamint Sink. Center, Governor Merriam, rifle in hand, rides as express messenger with Driver Ollie Dearborn on Mt. Whitney-Death Valley stage. Lower, Sam Ball, veteran desert prospector, hands gourd of water from Lake Tulainyo to Gov. Merriam while descendants of survivors of Jayhawker Party look on. Left to right, Henry and Frank Doty, sons of Capt. Ed Doty of Jayhawkers; Mrs. Melissa Lindner and E.W. Mecum, secretary of Jayhawker Association. November, 1937.

Power shovel at Echo Summit making a cut for the Meyers grade relocation (US 50). This 2.3 mile long unit was constructed under the direction of the U.S. Bureau of Public Roads at an approximate cost of $303,000. August, 1938.

Excavation underway on the Newhall cut (Rte. 23) being developed for the purpose of eliminating the Newhall Tunnel through the Newhall Range of mountains. Only 17.5 feet in width, the tunnel constituted a major traffic bottleneck. November, 1938.

Deep trenches to be backfilled with rock for drainage and, thus increased stability in the Santa Cruz Mountains. October, 1938.

Yuba Pass highway maintenance station, 1938.

Highway excavation of a 210' deep cut at Oregon Mountain (Trinity County) by hydraulicking. The white broken line shows the highway grade through the cut at the summit. The project required the construction of a 3,750,000 gallon reservoir. A total of 10,748,000 cubic yards were moved over five years using this unique procedure. The project was completed on June 30, 1939.

Erosion control of embankment on the Angeles Crest Highway by brush layering using prison labor, 1938.

CHAPTER 4

THE FREEWAY ERA 1940-1969

"Freeways are here to stay. The California Highway Commission is empowered to declare additional freeways and the engineers are prepared to design and construct them. The progress of ultimate future construction, however, will depend on public reaction. If the traveling public finds freeways to their advantage... the ultimate future of freeways is unlimited."

Frank W. Clark, Director of Public Works, January 1941

1940 ushered in a period of dormancy in the highway construction program, due to World War II, followed by over thirty years during which an unparalleled level of construction activity was initiated and maintained. The accomplishments of this period were made possible by California's rapid growth, the development of an adequate and predictable source of highway funding, and, of course, the federal Interstate program.

In 1939, the California Legislature passed a critically important piece of legislation establishing the freeway as a means of public conveyance. The law restricted freeway access from abutting properties and authorized the alteration or closing of local roads and streets intersecting freeways by means of "freeway agreements."

Within two weeks of the date the law went into effect, the California Highway Commission approved the first group of freeway declarations involving thirty-four miles of highway.

On December 30, 1940, the West's first freeway, the Arroyo Seco Parkway between Pasadena and Los Angeles, was opened. The benefits, in terms of improved traffic flow, were immediately apparent.

As the United States drifted toward participation in World War II in 1940-41, a national policy evolved to significantly reduce highway construction in order to conserve materials necessary for an ongoing defense build up. In accordance with the Defense Highway Act of 1941, the highest priority was given to the Defense Highway System as approved by the Secretary of War. Approximately $1,000,000 was approved for California defense highways. The priorities established by the newly constituted War Production Board largely limited highway construction to defense plant access roads, defense highways, and projects deemed essential to the defense effort.

With the implementation of gasoline rationing after the outbreak of war in December, 1941, gasoline tax revenues fell sharply (50% in the first year).

This, plus federal restrictions and a major reduction in available manpower, resulted in a highway program consisting primarily of minimal maintenance. As a result of the much heavier volume of truck traffic generated by the war effort, pavements deteriorated at a rapid rate. What little highway construction that was undertaken during the war years often involved the use of scrap materials such as old railroad rails in lieu of reinforcing steel.

Anticipating a major highway program at the war's end, the 1943 Legislature appropriated $12,000,000 for surveys and the preparation of plans and specifications. In 1944, the California Highway Commission recommended a major post-war highway construction program of 145 individual projects at an estimated cost of $80,000,000.

Even with the increased federal aid expenditures provided by the Federal Aid Highway Act of 1944, it became apparent that funding for post-war highway construction would not meet the demand resulting from the anticipated large increases in traffic volume. In 1947, in response to the recommendations of the Joint Interim Committee on Highways, Roads, Streets and Bridges, the Legislature passed the Collier-Burns Act after a lengthy and bitter legislative battle. Because of his successful shepherding of this fundamentally important bill through the Legislature, Senator Collier has often been referred to as "Father of the Freeways." Some of the key provisions of this act, which placed California's highway program on a sound financial basis, included:

- Adding 67 miles of city streets to the state highway system
- Consolidating county road administration
- Requiring that the state maintain state highways in cities
- Increasing gasoline and diesel fuel taxes from 3 to 4.5 cents per gallon
- Increasing automobile registration fees from $3.00 to $6.00, with a proportional increase in weight taxes on trucks
- Creating a fund into which all highway revenues and excess motor vehicle taxes would be deposited

- Revising apportionments of revenues from fuel taxes to cities, counties and the state

- Dividing state highway construction funds with 55% allocated to the southern and 45% to the northern counties.

A further two-year augmentation of gas tax revenues was enacted by the 1953 Legislature. The gasoline tax was increased from 4.5 to 7 cents per gallon. For this same period, the other highway user taxes were increased by a third. These increases were extended to 1960 by the 1955 Legislature and made permanent in 1959.

Without question, the most important single piece of national highway legislation to that time was enacted by Congress in 1956. The Federal-Aid Highway Act provided for the funding and construction of 40,000 miles of interstate highway to be designated the "National System of Interstate and Defense Highways." The funding level for this vast undertaking was established at $25,000,000,000 over a thirteen year period with increased funding for primary and secondary highways. The primary funding source, as provided by the Highway Revenue Act, was the imposition of a three cent per gallon federal gasoline tax. The act further provided that the revenues from the gas tax and other federal highway user taxes were to be deposited into a "Highway Trust Fund." The federal share of Interstate construction cost was set at 90% as compared to the previous 50-50 basis for federal aid projects. This landmark legislation set into motion the largest highway building program of all time.

At the request of the 1957 Legislature, the Division of Highways submitted a plan for a statewide freeway and expressway system to include city streets and county roads. It proposed the construction of 12,241 miles of controlled access highways serving every city with a population greater than 5,000 and carrying over half of all motor vehicle traffic. This plan served as the basis for legislation enacted during the 1959 legislative session.

The Collier-Unruh Local Transportation Act, enacted in 1963, provided for a further one-cent per gallon increase in the gasoline tax with proportional increases in user fees. The revenues generated were to be dedicated to county and city roads.

With a secure, adequate and predictable source of funding in place, state and federal legislative mandates, and the pressure of unprecedented traffic growth, California embarked on a massive highway construction program for the next two decades, during which the bulk of the state's highway system was constructed or upgraded. During this period, many records in volume of construction work were set, many of which still stand. For example, in 1960, bids were received for a record 13,257,327 square feet of bridges as compared to the approximate 3,500,000 per year in the early 1990's. This differential reflects the transition begun in the late 1960's from the construction of new facilities to the rehabilitation and upgrading of the existing system.

Among the many projects constructed between 1940 and 1969 were the Bayshore, Golden State, Cabrillo, San Diego, Santa Monica, Eastshore and Embarcadero freeways, to name a few. Among the many structures built in support of this program were the Antler, Richmond-San Rafael, Carquinez, Benicia-Martinez, San Diego-Coronado, San Mateo-Haward and Vincent Thomas bridges. In addition, a considerable effort was expended on exploratory and preliminary design work for a proposed southern crossing in the San Francisco bay area.

Innovation in highway technology flourished in California during this period. In 1942, the still widely used California Bearing Ratio (CBR) method of pavement design was introduced. It was replaced in 1951 by the "R-value" procedure. Both procedures were developed by the Materials and Research Department of the Division of Highways. Other developments included improved bank protection and erosion control, slip form paving of concrete pavements, concrete traffic barriers, prestressed concrete bridges, electrical traffic monitors, and sand drains.

Natural disasters in the form of the northern California floods of 1955 and 1964 took their toll on the highway program as did the inevitable slides, the most notable of which occurred at Orinda (Rte. 75) in 1951 and Pinole (US 80) in 1969. However, for reasons of the convergence of adequate funding, public support, state and federal legislative mandates, and the skill and dedication of state and contractor personnel, the period from 1940 to 1969 could justifiably be considered the "Golden Age" of the California highway program.

Pioneering a 134' cut in Mint Canyon cut-off grading operations. This project resulted in a savings of 5.2 miles to the users of the Mint Canyon Highway in Los Angeles County (US 6 and US 395). Built under four separate contracts, it involved 1,520,000 cubic yards of excavation. March, 1940.

The Brighton Test Track in Sacramento, in operation from 1940 to 1942, in which varying thicknesses of pavement materials were tested to destruction under heavy truck traffic. The test, conducted by the Materials and Research Department, provided the basis of the Division of Highways' pavement design procedure.

A 400' slip-out on US 101 north of Cloverdale. The record rain storms of February 25-29, 1940 resulted in an estimated $16,000,000 in damage to highways, levees and agricultural land in northern California.

A bulldozer engaged in precarious slide prevention work on Rte. 1 north of Santa Monica, 1940.

A military convoy shares a 2 lane highway with civilian traffic illustrating the problems on the existing highway system resulting from the defense build up, 1940.

An old timber truss bridge that collapsed under a truck and trailer loaded with a power shovel, both vehicles being considerably over the posted weight limit. The truck and fallen span lie in shallow water. November, 1940.

"The First Freeway in the West," The Arroyo-Seco Parkway is opened on December 30, 1940.

Highway bridge across the Sacramento River at Antler made necessary by the relocation of US 99 due to the construction of Shasta Dam. It is a steel deck truss structure 1330' in length with a concrete deck 210' above the river. 1941.

Redwood timber deflectors used for bank protection on the Eel River. The minimum 24" diameter logs were used for the deflectors which were 60' apart and extended into the river 100' from center line. 1941.

Army engineers inspect a test pavement at Stockton Field after a conference on the California Bearing Ratio (CBR) method of pavement design in Sacramento in April, 1942. The CBR procedure, developed by O.J. Porter of the Materials and Research Department, was ultimately adopted by the army for wartime runway and highway pavement design. It remains the most widely used pavement design procedure in the world today.

Traffic circle at the intersection of Lakewood Blvd. and Coast Highway near Long Beach. Completed at a cost of $31,262 in April, 1942, it served to eliminate a severe bottleneck generated by the burgeoning defense industry in the area.

Automatic broken line traffic stripping equipment developed by the Headquarters Shop in operation on a state highway, 1942.

Dynamiting packed snow at Sonora Pass to reopen Rte. 108, 1942.

Necessity is the mother of invention (or innovation). At left, the old Salmon River Bridge. At right, as it appeared rebuilt with salvaged steel as a result of wartime restrictions, 1943.

As a result of wartime restrictions, this 1100-gallon oil distributor was built with used parts from other units by the Headquarters Shop. Construction of equipment with salvaged materials became a standard practice during the war. 1943.

Push profilograph, developed by the Materials and Research Department to quantify pavement ride quality, 1944.

Experimental "mudjacking" equipment in operation. The procedure involves forcing cement-treated loam under concrete pavement slabs to reduce step-off between slabs and to fill voids. 1944.

The Albion River Bridge in Mendocino County, built at a cost of $350,000 with mostly salvaged materials, 1944.

Planning the post-war highway construction program. From left to right, G.T. McCoy, State Highway Engineer, Senator Randolph Collier, Charles W. Lyon, Speaker of the Assembly, and F.J. Grumm, Assistant State Highway Engineer, 1946.

Experimental use of a machine developed by Hurst Lewis of Los Angeles to cut weakened plane joints in newly poured concrete pavement at 15' intervals, 1946.

Subsealing of concrete pavement slabs with air-blown asphalt heated to 350-400 degrees F., a practice which was ultimately stopped due to safety considerations, 1946.

A Division of Highways traffic checker involved in an "Origin and Destination" study on a Bay Area highway under the close surveillance of the driver's dog. These studies provide the basis for the prediction of future traffic needs. 1947.

The old posted (16-ton maximum) Slick Rock Bridge in Mendocino County replaced by a 168' long arch culvert and fill, 1947.

An experimental concrete traffic deflector placed on the 6% Grapevine Grade on US 99 in the late fall of 1946. The 2000' long barrier was installed in an effort to reduce the high maintenance costs of metal guard rails and the prevention of collisions. This grade was notorious for run-away truck accidents. 1947.

Cabrillo Freeway in Mission Valley, San Diego County, under construction, 1947.

H-piling being stored at a Division of Highways, Service and Supply facility in Sacramento, available for loan to contractors to expedite construction, 1949.

The recently completed Three-Mile Slough Bridge on Rte. 24 near Rio Vista. The towers on the lift span are 155' above the water. 1949.

A portable, 115-ton capacity, pile load tester developed by the Bridge Department of the Division of Highways, 1950.

Blasting through Piru Gorge. This spectacular explosion on the Ridge Route, the result of explosives placed in 350 holes, was in support of the widening of US 99 from 2 to 4 lanes and the development of a new channel for Piru Creek, 1950.

The first prestressed reinforced concrete girder used in California is hoisted onto abutments of the Arroyo Seco Parkway Pedestrian Overcrossing in March, 1951. Prestressing, which originated in Europe, permits significant reductions in the use of reinforcing steel and makes longer concrete spans economical.

The first prestressed bridge in the west and the second in the U.S., the pedestrian overcrossing of the Arroyo Seco flood channel was completed in 1951. This project ushered in an era during which prestressed concrete became the dominant material for bridge spans.

FACING PAGE: The Orinda slide of December, 1950 which closed Rte. 75. It involved a mass of earth 300' in width and extended up the hillside a distance of 800'. Slide correction involved drying the slide mass with 95 horizontal drains, plus slope flattening.

Aerial view of the newly completed Pacheco Pass Highway showing the contrast between the new and old alignments, 1951.

The first unit of the Bayshore Freeway in San Francisco, between Alemany Blvd. and Army St., which was dedicated on June 1, 1951.

The Colorado Street Freeway Bridge over the Arroyo Seco, under construction. The $3,389,650 contract, awarded to the Guy F. Atkinson Company in the spring of 1951, was the largest ever awarded at that time by the Division of Highways. 1952.

The 9.85-mile long section of the Eastshore Freeway between Warm Springs and San Jose under construction in January, 1953. Looking north on the freeway at the Coyote Creek Bridge.

The heart of the Los Angeles metropolitan freeway system, the first four-level direct connector interchange structure in the world, at the intersection of the Hollywood, Santa Ana, Pasadena, and Harbor freeways, 1953.

Gaviota Pass Tunnel in Santa Barbara County under construction in January, 1953. The $3,300,000 project was one of several to ultimately provide a limited access freeway between Gaviota and one mile north of Nojoqui Summit.

The Richmond-San Rafael Bridge under construction in March, 1953. The new San Francisco Bay crossing, financed by a California Toll Bridge Authority Bond Issue of $72,000,000 would have an over-water length of 4.0 miles. The substructure contract provided for 79 concrete piers supported on H piles. The double-decked structure would have six traffic lanes.

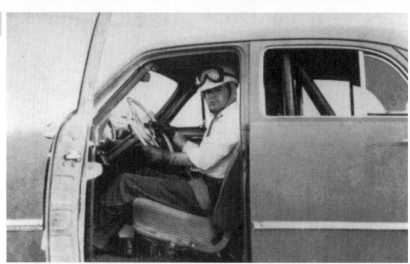

Early crash tests by the Materials and Research Department were conducted with test drivers rather than the presently used elastomeric dummies, a practice which would probably be troubling to OSHA. Test driver E.W. Kessinger in May, 1954.

Open water fill across Candlestick Cove for the Bayshore Freeway (US 101) constructed by the displacement of soft bay mud, 1955.

The Mad River Bridge partially destroyed by the floods of the winter of 1955-1956 in northern California.

Camels lead the Banning and Beaumont High School bands at the dedication of the reconstruction and widening of 5.2 miles of US 60 on February 16, 1956.

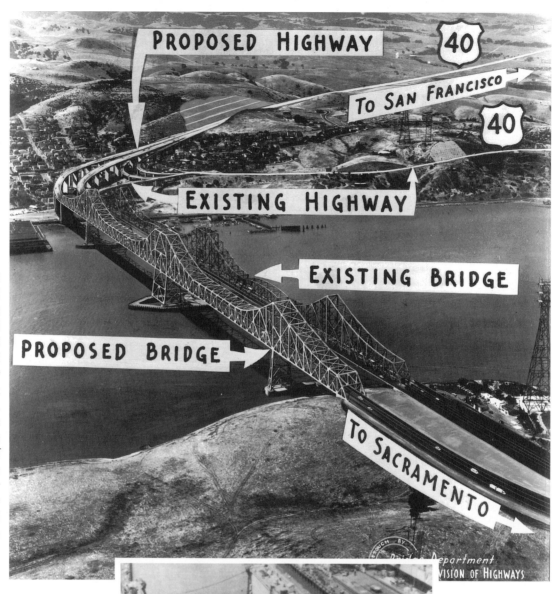

PROPOSED HIGHWAY

40

TO SAN FRANCISCO

40

EXISTING HIGHWAY

EXISTING BRIDGE

PROPOSED BRIDGE

TO SACRAMENTO

Bridge Department
VISION OF HIGHWAYS

The proposed additional Carquinez Straits Bridge, authorized by Senate Bill 1450 which was signed by Governor Goodwin J. Knight on June 16, 1955. Provision was made for the issuance of $73,000,000 in revenue bonds for its construction by the California Toll Bridge Authority.

Erection of the 53' by 102' caisson for Pier 2 of the parallel Carquinez Bridge at the Bethlehem Pacific Coast Shipbuilding drydock in San Francisco, underway in September, 1956.

California's first double-decked freeway, the Cypress Street Viaduct in Oakland, is opened to traffic on June 11, 1957. This 1.5 mile unit of the Eastshore Freeway connected the Bay Bridge Distribution Structure with the southerly extension of the Eastshore Freeway. An 8 lane structure, it was built under two contracts at a cost of approximately $8,500,000. Its partial collapse during the 1989 Loma Prieta earthquake alerted the engineering world to the shortcoming of the pre-1971 design codes. A nation-wide program of strengthening older bridges was then initiated.

San Francisco's Embarcadero Freeway under construction in January, 1957. The foreground shows progress toward the Embarcadero. The Main and Beale St. ramps are in the center.

Redwood Highway construction in Humboldt County, September, 1957. Four scrapers are being winched up the ramp of the "big cut" simultaneously by four donkey engines.

Stress and strain measurements underway to test a steel strand for use in prestressed concrete bridges, by the Structural Materials Section of the Materials and Research Department, 1957.

A successful horizontal drain installation in San Luis Obispo County in 1958, using a drill rig designed and built by personnel of the Materials and Research and Equipment Departments.

Driving home a large steel pin at a girder expansion hinge during the construction of the Carquinez Bridge, 1958.

The Carquinez Bridge complete and open to traffic as of November 25, 1958. The "big cut" on the southerly approach (background), the world's largest to that time, involved 8,800,000 cubic yards of excavation. It is 2500' long, 1370 wide and 300' deep at its deepest point.

Modeling the East Los Angeles Freeway Interchange. The use of models of complex interchanges became a standard practice in the 1950s in order to identify design problems and to review the aesthetics of a given design. 1958.

Governor Edmond G. Brown depositing the first quarter in one of the new automatic toll takers on the San Francisco-Oakland Bay Bridge Toll Plaza, May 21, 1959.

Public hearing on a proposed highway routing in the Stockton area. These public meetings are open for all interested individuals and organizations in order to obtain their views on the results of engineering and environmental studies of project alternatives. 1959.

The first slipform paving operation on a Division of Highways project in the metropolitan Los Angeles area. This new procedure for the placement of concrete pavement eliminated the need for side forms secured with steel pins. 1960.

Seismic refraction testing for the Antelope Valley Freeway (Rte. 14). Based upon the measurement of the velocity of sound waves generated by a sharp blow or explosion, seismic testing data permit an estimate of whether ripping or blasting will be necessary for a given excavation. 1960.

Survey underway for the relocation of US 40 (now I-80) at Donner Summit, 1960.

Foundation drilling operation in Orange County to obtain soil samples for testing, 1960.

Concrete columns for the first section of the Santa Monica Freeway (I-10) westward from the East Los Angeles Interchange, 1961.

Crash test of chain link barrier fence by the Materials and Research Department with a remote controlled vehicle and an instrumented dummy passenger, 1961.

San Francisco-Oakland Bay Bridge maintenance painting. This crew works the year around. When they finish, it's time to start over. 1961.

Benicia-Martinez Bridge under construction. The concrete stem, which rises 100' to 130' above the footing, is placed by the "slip form" method at a rate of 10" per hour. 1961.

A portion of I-15 known as "Baker Grade." Work on the conversion of this highway to a full freeway was completed in September, 1961.

Snow avalanche control on US 50 west of Echo Summit by a National Guard gun crew using a 105mm recoilless rifle, 1962.

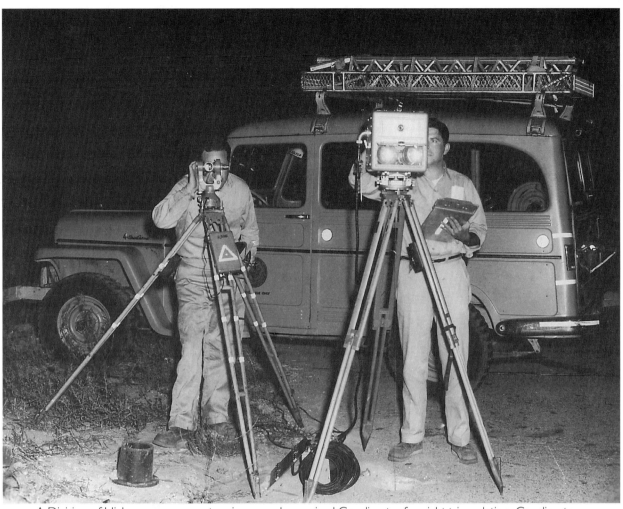

A Division of Highways survey party using a newly acquired Geodimeter for night triangulation. Geodimeters permit a precise distance measurement by the indirect determination of the time required for a pulsed light beam to travel between 2 stations. 1962.

Caldecott Tunnel on Rte. 24 (Alameda County) construction, April, 1962.

Benicia-Martinez ferry service ends with the opening of the new toll bridge on September 15, 1962.

The newly completed Benicia-Martinez Toll Bridge just west of the movable span. Southern Pacific railway bridge is visible in the foreground, 1962.

The Vincent Thomas Bridge between San Pedro and Terminal Island in Los Angeles Harbor under construction. The photo shows the cable spinning operation which was completed in December, 1962.

Marilyn Reece, the first woman to become an associate highway engineer with the Division of Highways, reviews the plans of the three-level San Diego (I-405)-Santa Monica (I-10) Freeway Interchange with Resident Engineer Thomas McKinley. Mrs. Reece had supervised the design of the project. 1963.

Grooving concrete pavement for improved skid resistance, 1963.

"Sierra Sam," the Materials and Research Department's anthropometric dummy loses his head in a bridge rail crash test, 1963.

Self-propelled pneumatic drills in operations on the solid granite of Donner Summit prior to blasting in the construction of I-80, 1962.

Steel Raising on the Vincent Thomas Bridge, March 12, 1963. The final preassembled panel of deck truss for the main span is being lifted from a barge with high strength cables.

Maintenance men south of Point Reyes changing a sign reflecting a newly adopted highway numbering system, 1964.

Technicians in the process of comparing the results of nuclear gauge moisture and density measurements with those from the conventional sand volume procedure. This study led to the adoption of the faster and more economical nuclear gauge method compaction control. 1964.

Cable carrier used to carry people and supplies across Canyon Creek near Junction City during the December, 1964 floods in northern California. Rte. 299 is in the background.

Martin's Ferry Bridge destroyed by the rampaging Klamath River in December, 1964. The top of the pier in the foreground, which is 95' above normal river flow, was found to have flood debris on it.

An army surplus Bailey bridge replaces a washed out span on the Smith River (US 199) in two months. The Bailey bridge system consists of many identical small members which can be easily transported and connected. It was developed for military use during World War II, 1965.

"Traveling Deflectometer" designed by engineers of the Materials and Research Department. In 1965 a pavement overlay design procedure based upon deflection measurements made with this device was adopted by the Division of Highways.

I-80 over the Sierras is opened in November, 1964 after 8 years of construction. Old US 40 and the historic Donner Summit arch bridge are visible in the foreground. To the right of US 40, the 1868 Central Pacific Railroad and traces of the 1864 Dutch Flat toll road are visible.

Hiel Avenue Pedestrian Overcrossing over I-405 in Orange County. This structure, which was constructed circa 1965, illustrates the versatility of the concrete box girder bridge for use on curves. The box girder type bridge was developed by Caltrans engineers in the mid 1940s.

A 3-lane (36' wide) slip form concrete paver in operation on a state highway project, 1965.

A girder for the Pioneer Memorial Bridge (Sacramento) is loaded onto a barge at the Napa Kaiser Steel Yard in 1965.

A 280' high fill on Rte. 152 contiguous to the San Luis Reservoir, part of the new 12-mile section which was opened April 29, 1965.

Opening a 25-mile stretch of I-5 in San Diego County with District Engineer Jacob Dekema riding shotgun, 1966.

Night concrete paving on a widening of the Long Beach Freeway. Begun on June 13, 1966, 26 miles of single lane pavement were placed in 16 working nights. Night paving eliminated interference from the heavy daytime traffic and permitted longer working shifts.

A tired but satisfied
U.C.L.A. student
archaeologist after a
"dig" on Highway 1
right-of-way north
of Cambria, 1966.

Girl Scouts engaged in a highway landscaping project in Los Angeles County, 1966.

Al Sequreia, an electrical engineer with the Materials and Research Department, measuring culvert distortion under a 167' high fill at Apple Canyon (I-5) in Los Angeles County, 1966. This research ultimately led to improved design procedures for culverts under high fills.

Division of Highways surveyor working on a rock face while staking for the realignment of Rte. 120 at Tioga Pass, 1966.

An inspector applies X-ray photo film to a welded area before making a radiographic check for hidden flaw, 1967.

Newly completed I-680 in Alameda County on a corridor shared by the Southern Pacific and Western Pacific railroads, 1967.

The Squaw Creek fill, the highest on the state highway system at 383', under construction on US 101 in Mendocino County, 1967.

The Westside Freeway (I-5) (right) and the California Aqueduct (left) under construction in 1967. In a cooperative agreement between the two state agencies involved, excavated material from aqueduct construction was often used for fill construction on this portion of I-5.

The San Diego-Coronado Toll Bridge under construction in 1968. The towers are supported by clusters of 54" prestressed concrete piling. The main spans are welded trapezoidal steel box girders.

The San Diego-Coronado Bridge complete, 1969.

The Pinole slipout of May, 1969, which temporarily closed 4 lanes of I-80.

THE ENVIRONMENTAL AND MULTI-MODAL ERA 1970-1995

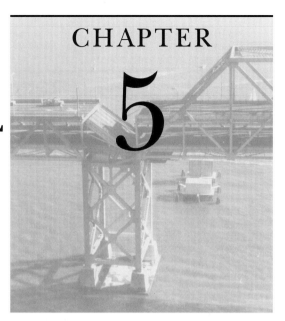

CHAPTER 5

"The department will endeavor to provide a degree of transportation mobility that is in balance with other values. It must ensure that economic, social, and environmental effects are fully considered along with technical issues in the development of transportation programs and projects so that final decisions are made in the best overall public interest."

Leo J. Trombatore, Director, California Department of Transportation – 1983

The year 1970 ushered in a chaotic and turbulent period of change to the Department of Public Works, soon to be the Department of Transportation (Caltrans). Some of the myriad of problems and challenges that confronted the Department were declining revenue, significantly increased construction and maintenance costs, a major reorganization, the "freeway revolt," environmental legislation at both the state and national levels, and the development of a state transportation plan.

In addition to the normal occurrence of slides and floods, three major earthquakes resulted in severe damage to the state's transportation system, which required major revisions in design criteria and the initiation of a massive bridge retrofit program.

Two pieces of legislation, enacted in 1969 and 1970 respectively, were to have a profound effect on the department's highway construction program. These were the National Environmental Policy Act (NEPA) and the California Environmental Quality Act (CEQA). In response, an environmental function was initiated within headquarters and districts. The environmental program rapidly became a significant part of the department's planning and design, construction, and maintenance efforts. Environmental staff provided expertise and training in the areas of air and water quality, hazardous waste, archaeology, historic preservation, and noise abatement.

The primary responsibility given to the department's environmental staff is the preparation of Environmental Impact Reports (EIR) on specific projects which identify potential environmental hazards and recommend appropriate mitigation. Another important function of environmental staff is to provide advice with respect to the continually increasing and changing environmental laws and regulations.

In the late 1960's, opposition to new freeway construction, the "freeway revolt," materialized throughout the United States including California, due to the belief of many groups and private citizens that planners and engineers were more concerned with the more efficient and timely movement of traffic than the negative environmental, social, and aesthetic effects of new freeways in their communities. An extreme example of this opposition in California was directed at the partially completed Embarcadero Freeway in San Francisco, which was ultimately demolished in 1991 after years of controversy.

In 1968, in response to this and other concerns, Governor Reagan established a twenty-four man task force to consider the state's role in transportation planning and a more responsive organizational structure. The task force's recommendation led to legislation establishing a State Transportation Board in 1969 and an Office of Transportation Planning and Research in 1970. The Board's first action was the initiation of a study of the need for a Department of Transportation. A separate organizational study was undertaken by an interdisciplinary staff task force working with McKinsey & Co. under the direction of the executive secretary of the State Transportation Board. What ultimately emerged as a result of these studies was a plan for the creation of a Department of Transportation from the merger of the Departments of Public Works and Aeronautics including the creation of two new divisions, Mass Transportation and Transportation Planning. The proposed reorganization, carried as AB 69, was passed and signed into law on December 14, 1972. The new Department of Transportation (Caltrans) was to consist of six functional and modal divisions: Highways, Mass Transportation, Aeronautics, Transportation Planning, Legal, and Administrative Services.

The legislation also assigned Caltrans the task of preparing a California Transportation Plan based upon input from regional transportation planning agencies and overall state objectives. Between 1975 and 1977, three draft transportation plans were submitted and rejected by the public and/or the Legislature for differing reasons. In 1978, the Legislature created the State Transportation Commission, assigning it fiscal control of the planning functions of the California Highway Commission and State Transportation Board. A budgeting process was adopted requiring a five year State Transportation Improvement Program (STIP) with input from local and regional government entities as the basis for programming state and regional projects. The STIP, which was required to be updated biennially, was to be, in effect, the State Transportation

Plan. The net effect of this legislation was increased input and control of state transportation policy and budgeting by the Legislature.

An endemic problem of the 1970-1995 era was that of financial support. Until 1968, fuel tax revenues had increased at a rate greater than that of inflation. By 1973, as a result of inflation and the OPEC oil embargo, fuel tax revenues were $130,000,000 lower than in 1968, while the decade of the '70s saw freeway construction costs increase by 190%.

These cost increases were due to the high inflation rates of that period, a significant upscaling of design standards, skyrocketing increases in urban land values, and the delays and mitigation made necessary by environmental and community concerns. The situation was exacerbated by the reluctance of the three successive administrations of Reagan, Brown and Deukmejian to seek an increase in fuel taxes. Highway financing was further constricted by passage of the "Gann Appropriations Limit" initiative in 1979, which restricted state appropriation growth increases to population growth or the increase in the Consumer Price Index, whichever was greater. Maintenance and construction costs had historically grown at twice the inflation rate. Thus, even with the two-cent increase reluctantly accepted by the Brown administration in 1981, California ranked last among the states in per capita spending for transportation in 1983.

In 1990, concerned with growing traffic congestion, California taxpayers approved a five-cent per gallon increase in the gasoline tax with a further increase of one-cent per year until 1994. Even so, the 1994 gasoline tax rate was well below the national average, due to the small increases between 1960 and 1990. Thus while some freeway gap closures and projects to increase capacity would be possible, with few exceptions, the program would concentrate on the upgrading, rehabilitation, and maintenance of the existing system with increased emphasis on mass transit.

On February 9, 1971, a Richter magnitude 6.6 seismic event, later to be known as the Sylmar earthquake, occurred in the north San Fernando Valley. It proved to be the first quake to cause major damage to freeway structures. Damage was concentrated on Interstate 5 from the Mission separation structure to the Santa Clara River overhead structure. Other roadways affected included Routes 14, 210, 2, and 405, which suffered settlement at bridge approaches, buckling and heaving of concrete pavement and some fill distortion. The most severe structural damage occurred within the limits of two ongoing construction contracts, the partially completed I-5/I-210 and I-5/Rte. 14 interchanges. This earthquake revealed that many of the design details commonly used by bridge engineers throughout the world were inadequate to resist the forces caused by a seismic event of this magnitude. These findings triggered a seismic retrofit program which is still underway. Also, significant changes were immediately made in the California bridge design standard for all future bridges. These new standards, which were developed primarily by Caltrans bridge engineers, were the basis for a new national bridge code.

In 1973, the Division of Mass Transportation (DMT) came into existence as a modal division of Caltrans. Its primary responsibility was to assist and encourage local governmental entities in the development of urban and regional mass transportation facilities, particularly in obtaining federal financial support through the Urban Mass

Transportation Agency (UMTA) of the U.S. Department of Transportation. UMTA grants for mass transit from the Highway Trust Fund were made possible by federal highway legislation in the mid 1970's The earliest example of a successful collaboration for the development of mass transit was that between DMT and the San Diego Metropolitan Development Board in the construction of a light rail facility from downtown San Diego to the Mexican border, popularly known as the "Tijuana Trolley" which was completed in 1981. Project assistance in design, construction inspection and right-of-way engineering were provided by Caltrans. Similar successes followed with the construction of light rail systems in Sacramento, Los Angeles and San Jose, all with the heavy involvement of Caltrans.

The second major earthquake of this period occurred on October 17, 1989. Centered in the Santa Cruz mountains, what was to become known as the "Loma Prieta" earthquake registered 7.1 on the Richter scale and resulted in extensive damage to the transportation system of the San Francisco Bay area. By far the most catastrophic result of the quake was the collapse of the Cypress Viaduct portion of I-880 in Oakland which resulted in forty-two deaths. A total of sixty five structures were damaged on the Bay area state highway and interstate system, eleven of which were closed. In addition, a section of the San Francisco-Oakland Bay Bridge collapsed. As a direct result of the Loma Prieta event, earthquake research by the Caltrans Division of Structures and several universities was accelerated. The bridge retrofit program entered a new phase which was concentrated on single column structures.

For reasons cited earlier, capital outlay for the period was concentrated on operational improvements of the existing system, pavement rehabilitation, sound wall construction, traffic safety improvements, and the retrofitting of structures. However, a number of large highway projects involving new alignment were completed, including I-680, the Ridge Route, the Westside Freeway, and the closure of the final gap on I-5.

The Redwood Park Bypass, begun in 1984, proved to be one of the most difficult earthmoving operations ever undertaken by Caltrans. Beginning approximately 50 miles north of Eureka, this realignment of US 101 consisted of twelve miles of four lane highway through extremely rugged and unstable terrain. It involved 12,000,000 cubic yards of earthwork and the placement of 750,000 tons of drain rock. It was completed in the fall of 1992 at an ultimate cost of approximately $130,000,000.

On October 14, 1993, the country's most costly highway, the 17.3 mile long Century Freeway from El Segundo to I-605 was opened. From start to finish, almost thirty years including ten years of litigation were required to complete it, as compared to the normal ten years for freeway construction. Its final cost was $2,200,000,000 including $670,000,000 for right-of-way acquisition, $360,000,000 for housing and $725,000,000 for a light rail system along the centerline. The cost and delay associated with the Century Freeway signalled, for all practical purposes, the end of urban freeway construction in California.

Major structures completed during this period included the Dumbarton, Antioch, and Pine Valley bridges, the I-110 High Occupancy Vehicle (HOV) Viaduct and the I-380/US 101 interchange.

Rising construction costs and declining revenue stimulated technical innovation in the areas of asphalt concrete recycling, movable traffic barriers, breakaway signs, energy attenuators, computer traffic simulation and computer aided design.

A pavement management system to prioritize pavement rehabilitation needs on a statewide basis was adopted by the Caltrans Division of Maintenance.

The third major earthquake of the period occurred on January 17, 1994. With an epicenter in the San Fernando Valley, this 6.7 Richter magnitude event, designated the "Northridge" earthquake, resulted in extensive damage to highway structures in the greater Los Angeles area. A total of 212 structures sustained damage, five of which collapsed, either partially or totally. One of America's busiest freeways, the Santa Monica (I-10) was closed. Those structures which had been retrofitted performed well, particularly those which had been modified based upon the results of research conducted subsequent to the Loma Prieta earthquake of 1989.

The last section of the new Ridge Route on I-5 was opened on August 24, 1970. This 43.2-mile, 8-lane primarily new alignment was the largest project ever undertaken by the Division of Highways to that time at $103,000,000. A unique solution to the problem presented by the rugged terrain was the use of separate alignments for each direction of travel, the northbound lanes crossing over the southbound lanes. This photo shows one of the two crossings.

Crash test of energy attenuators consisting of sand filled barrels by the Materials and Research Department, September 4, 1970. These devices, also called "crash cushions," are placed so as to stop errant vehicles headed for a solid obstruction, such as a bridge column, with minimal injury to seat-belted passengers.

Maintenance forces clear rockfall off US 50 at Echo Summit, 1971.

Newly completed safety roadside rest at Trinidad on US 101 in Humboldt County, 1971. The California Safety Roadside Rest Area System was authorized by the Legislature in 1963. At the present time, 88 rest area units serve approximately 90 million visitors annually.

Desert turtle relocation project near China Lake for the purpose of mitigating the environmental impact of a desert freeway, 1971.

Director of Public Works James Moe, on the left, touring earthquake damage in Los Angeles resulting from the Sylmar earthquake of February 9, 1971.

Concrete pavement buckling resulting from the Sylmar earthquake near the I-5/Rte. 14 separation, February 9, 1971.

Railroad track distortion caused by the Sylmar earthquake, 1971.

Collapsed I-210/Rte. 14/I-5 partially completed interchange structure as a result of the Sylmar earthquake, February 9, 1971.

Sign in support of the construction of the Century Freeway. Referendum conducted in May, 1971 by the City of Hawthorne.

Relief depicting the "Old Oregon Trail" on a Rte. 299 overcrossing in Shasta County which illustrates a greater concern for aesthetics by highway designers, 1973.

"In with the new, out with the old." The Caltrans and Division of Highways logos on maintenance equipment, 1973.

Diamond (carpool) lanes on the Santa Monica Freeway (I-10). Use of these lanes was restricted to vehicles with three or more passengers to encourage carpooling. Placed in operation in March, 1976, they were made available for mixed traffic twenty-one weeks later largely as a result of vehement public opposition.

The newly completed Pine Valley Bridge on I-8 in San Diego County, 1975. This was the second, and, by far, the largest bridge to be designed for construction by the segmental balanced cantilever method (falsework not used).

Crash Test of a break-away light standard by the Materials and Research Department in August, 1978. Based upon the results of tests such as this, breakaway signs and light standards were adopted on the State Highway System because of the reduced chance of injury to vehicle occupants.

Dedication of the final link of I-5 near Stockton on October 12, 1979. Director of Transportation Adrianna Gianturco, second from the left, is flanked by representatives of the Canadian and Mexican governments.

The "Tijuana Trolley" between San Diego and the Mexican Border. This light rail project, which was designed and constructed with heavy Caltrans involvement, was opened in July, 1981. It has an average daily ridership of 11,500.

The Malibu Slide of the spring of 1979 which temporarily closed the Coast Highway between Malibu and Santa Monica and generated a considerable amount of controversy. It was ultimately corrected by the removal of the most dangerous slide debris and by rock bolting.

One of several "tire anchored timber walls" designed by Caltrans to utilize recycled materials. This one has a facing of surplus railroad ties with tire sidewalls as the earthwork reinforcement. It was completed in 1983 on Rte. 1 in Santa Cruz County.

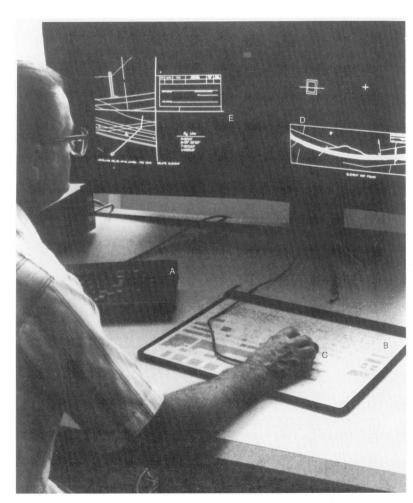

A Caltrans engineer engaged in computer-aided design, 1984.

The new Dumbarton Bridge, completed in October, 1983, utilized prestressed lightweight concrete box girders with welded steel box girders for the longer central spans. This allowed longer spans and a reduced number of supporting piers. The approach embankments to the 7400' structure were constructed with a number of innovative construction techniques including paper wick drains to accelerate the settlement of the soft bay mud, lightweight (sawdust fill) and geomembrane reinforcement.

An increasingly common sight in the 1980's: women in blue collar jobs.

A critically important and
sometimes dangerous
responsibility of Caltrans'
maintenance crews, clearing
urban freeways of accidents
such as this overturned rig
on I-5 in Los Angeles, 1987.

Aerial view of the
Century Freeway (I-105)
in the early stages of its
construction, 1987. The
photo shows the new
freeway crossing the
Harbor Freeway (I-110)
in the foreground.

Engineer/frogmen of Caltrans Structures Maintenance inspect the footings of a 60 year old bridge which carries Rte. 49 over the Middle Fork of the Yuba River, 1987.

The Redwood Park Bypass (US 101), a 12-mile-long, 4-lane highway which begins just north of Orick, under construction in 1988. Involving 12,000,000 cubic yards of earthmoving, the Park Bypass, from a stability and environmental standpoint, was one of the most difficult ever attempted by Caltrans or its predecessor organizations.

A giant viaduct on the Redwood Park Bypass project which carries the highway 100 feet over Boyes Creek, under construction in 1988. Such structures were necessary for an alignment free of sharp curves without massive cuts and fills.

An example of the effective use of surplus space controlled by Caltrans by its Division of Right of Way is the EZ-8 Motel in San Diego. In 1987, Caltrans realized $16,000,000 by leasing space within its right-of-way.

Rte. 85 under construction in 1988. This 6-lane freeway was funded by a 1/2 cent sales tax approved by the citizens of Santa Clara County in 1984. It represents a joint effort by the California Transportation Commission, the Santa Clara Traffic Authority, and Caltrans District 4.

Field demonstration of a movable median barrier in 1989. The transfer and transport vehicle, manufactured by Barrier Systems, Inc., can move the 1600-pound concrete barrier segments laterally more than one lane width at a speed of 6 miles per hour. A movable median barrier system is presently being used on the San Diego-Coronado Bridge.

Caltrans Maintenance tunnel washer at work on the Caldecott Tunnel in 1989. Like many special maintenance machines, this rig was designed and built by personnel of the Caltrans Equipment Shop.

The I-380/US 101 interchange, completed in 1987, in San Mateo County connects two interstate freeways to San Francisco International Airport enabling the heavily traveled US 101 motorists to avoid airport generated traffic.

The collapsed Cypress Street Viaduct, resulting from the Loma Prieta Earthquake of October 17, 1989.

Struve Slough Bridge on Rte. 1 near Watsonville. Support pilings have punched through the collapsing state highway as a result of the Loma Prieta Earthquake. Skid marks indicate where a police car avoided the pile stubs when responding at high speed immediately after the quake.

The collapse of a 50' section of the San Francisco-Oakland Bay Bridge resulting from the shear failure of 24 one-inch bolts. Caltrans engineers estimated the failure was caused by two million pounds of force generated by the Loma Prieta Earthquake.

Kay Griffin, Caltrans Office Engineer, flanked by E. Robert Ferguson of the Kasler Corporation (left) and Don Watson, Deputy Director (right), signs the biggest public works contract ever executed in California for the construction of I-105/I-405 Interchange ($134,000,000) in the fall of 1989.

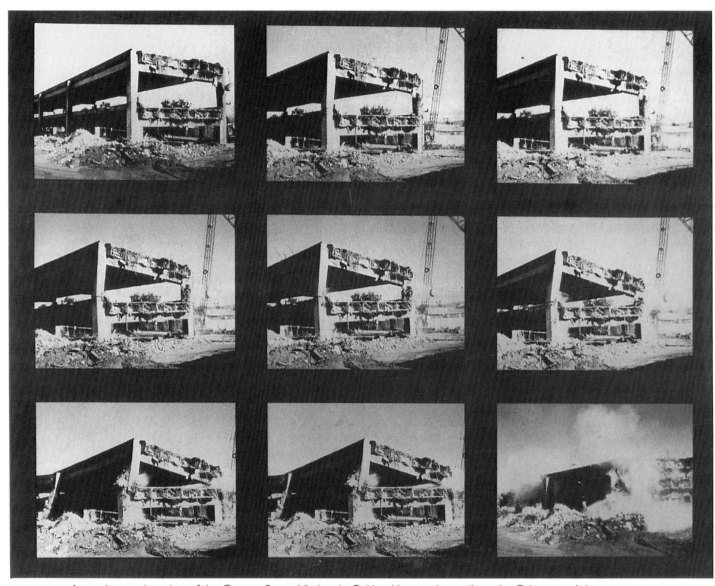

An undamaged section of the Cypress Street Viaduct in Oakland is tested to collapse by Caltrans and the University of California, Berkeley to verify earthquake retrofit designs, 1990.

Emergency ferry service inaugurated during the repair of earthquake damage to the San Francisco-Oakland Bay Bridge, October, 1989.

Clint Myers, owner of C.C. Myers Inc. receives a $1,000,000 bonus for the completion of two 800' spans over Struve Slough on Rte. 1 near Watsonville in just 55 days. Presenting the check is Resident Engineer Ramin Abidi, 1990.

Cold asphalt concrete recycling paving train, including a planer, crusher, mixer and blender, at work on Gilman Road in Shasta County. Its production capability at a depth of 2" to 4" was 4 lane miles per day, 1990.

The newly completed light rail line from Long Beach to downtown Los Angeles otherwise known as the "Blue Line", 1990.

The Sutter Square Galleria, a major shopping and office center built entirely on leased Caltrans property. The ground floor passes under and the four story portions straddle the elevated I-80 freeway in Sacramento, 1990.

A Bay Area Rapid Transit (BART) train pulls into a stop along a corridor shared with Caltrans. The passage of Proposition 111 in 1990 provided for significant increases in funding and flexibility for local mass transit improvements.

An automated pavement marker truck developed jointly by the University of California, Davis and Caltrans for the installation of raised traffic markers ("Botts Dots") more rapidly, effectively, and with greater safety, 1990.

A computer traffic simulator developed jointly by Caltrans, the California Polytechnic University (San Luis Obispo) and the California Highway Patrol, which allows trainees to deal with traffic congestion resulting from multiple causes, 1990.

Volunteers of the "Adopt A Highway" program engaged in litter clean up along a state highway, 1991.

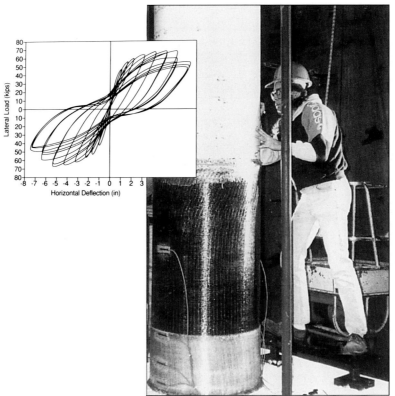

Bridge earthquake retrofit research involving fiber composite column jackets to increase the ductility of existing bridge columns, being conducted at the University of California, San Diego, 1991.

A productive archaeological dig, conducted by a team of Caltrans and San Jose State archaeologists from November 1989 until May 1990, the future site of a Caltrain light rail station in Santa Clara County.

Night maintenance crew at work on the Pasadena Freeway in Los Angeles, 1991.

Caltrans geologists monitor the earth-borne vibrations from a shear wave generator in order to predict the response of the site to a major earthquake, 1991.

District 07 Traffic Operations Center in Los Angeles. Traffic flow is closely monitored so that traffic snarls can be quickly eliminated. 1992.

Night sound wall construction on Rte. 91 in Orange County in 1993. The Caltrans Community Noise Abatement Program was initiated in 1974. By mid 1988, over 125 miles of soundwall had been constructed at a cost of $115,000,000.

District 5 Director Tom Pollock and Santa Barbara Mayor Sheila Lodge turn off the last traffic signal light on US 101 between San Francisco and Los Angeles in November, 1991, made possible by completion of Santa Barbara's crosstown freeway.

To counter a threat to US 101 by the meandering Mad River in Humboldt County, rock slope protection backed by geotextile fabric is placed along the toe of the highway embankment for a distance of 1300'. 1992.

Caltrans maintenance personnel engaged in a biennial survey of ride quality and pavement condition of all 48,000 lane miles of the State Highway System for input into the Pavement Management System. The resulting data plus traffic volume are used to develop state wide priorities for pavement rehabilitation. 1992.

The I-110 High Occupancy Vehicle (HOV) Viaduct under construction in 1993. The 7000' long prestressed concrete structure is supported in the median of the Harbor Freeway (I-110) in Los Angeles.

Collapsed section of the La Cienega-Venice Undercrossing of the Santa Monica Freeway (I-10) resulting from the Northridge earthquake of January 17, 1994.

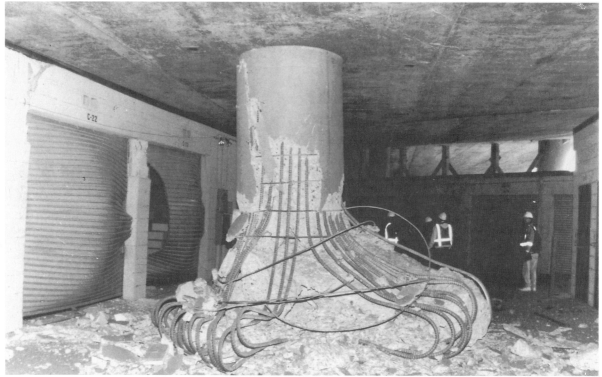

Typical column buckling of a non-retrofitted pre-1971 column due to insufficient confining steel at the La Cienega-Venice Undercrossing of the Santa Monica Freeway (I-10). Note that the spans collapsed onto the private mini-storage facility beneath the bridge.

Seismic retrofit of a critical structural element, a single column bent. Here, the column is encased by a steel jacket after which it will be welded closed. Cement grout can then be pumped into any void between the jacket and column. Caltrans accelerated its seismic retrofit program significantly after the Loma Prieta Earthquake of 1989.

Looking southwest from abutment 1 at the collapsed 2 spans of the north connector overcrossing of the Rte. 14/I-5 interchange.

Governor Pete Wilson speaking at the reopening of the Santa Monica Freeway (I-10) in April, 1994. Clint Myers (2nd from the left) of C.C. Myers Inc. realized a bonus of $15,000,000 for completing the project 74 days ahead of schedule.

The Centennial Ceremony on April 11, 1995 celebrated the 100th Anniversary of the founding of the Bureau of Highways. In a procession around the Capitol Mall in Sacramento, Caltrans Director James van Loben Sels and Caltrans Centennial Chairman Norman Root ride in a Wells Fargo stage coach.

EPILOGUE

On the occasion of the one hundredth anniversary of the founding of the Bureau of Highways, ultimately to become Caltrans, it is fitting to look back with pride and amazement at the achievements of the last century in the design and construction of one of the world's premier transportation systems. This system has contributed much to the development of the world's eighth ranking economy, the State of California. It represents a monument to the governmental agencies and contractors involved and, most importantly, the people of California.